COUNTING BLESSINGS

COUNTING BLESSINGS

Morris Berman

The Oliver Arts & Open Press
New York

ISBN: 978-0-9883343-6-6
Library of Congress Control Number: 2016940582
Cover design by John Trotter
Front cover: author with grandfather, 1949; photographer unknown.
Author photo by John Trotter

The Oliver Arts & Open Press, LLC
2578 Broadway (Suite #102)
New York, NY 10025
www.oliveropenpress.com

Counting Blessings was originally published in 2011 by the Cervená Barva
Press, W. Somerville, Massachusetts

FOREWORD by Paul Christensen

The first time I heard about Morris Berman was from a scruffy-looking graduate student whom I could count on for interesting talk in the hallway. He mentioned *The Reenchantment of the World* (1981) and thought I would "get it." I told him I'd take a look. That one book may have done more to clarify the post-Renaissance world to me than the several hundred books I had read with a similar wide reach over the previous ten years. My interests were in experimental poetry of the 20th century, especially the work of Charles Olson and Gary Snyder, Robert Creeley and Robert Duncan, where many of the ideas that later entered into the "theory revolution" in this country were first circulated. Olson coined the term "postmodern" in a letter from around 1950, and the "waterfall of destruction" of biodiversity was already in ink in Snyder's essays from the early 1960s. From as far back as Ezra Pound's "Imagism" of 1910, the thrust of poetry was toward re-animating the object, recognizing its soul so that nature could resume its real place in human affairs as a partner to reality and human conduct.

But since no one read poetry anymore, these incendiary notions went largely unheard until late in the century. And even then, critics didn't acknowledge the real sources of these ideas, but made it seem part of some profound upheaval within the academy, among those reading Foucault and Derrida, Paul De Man and Lyotard. Berman's *Reenchantment* interpreted the world after 1400 as a sudden shrinking of reality around human priorities, and the wide-spread witch burnings, heresy trials, wars of religion, and the rise of secular government all pointed the way toward an illusory rationality in which the planet was hacked to pieces for its resources. But a change occurred at the turn of the 20th century that began to restore something of the vision of the world before Dante. Einstein's relativity and the mysterious interactions of quantum physics put matter back into an equation with energy, or spirit, in which mass and body and the mud and rock of earth were one phase of a continuous cycle of interchange with spirit. Suddenly, the hierarchy of mind and spirit over the material world collapsed and an old and mystical dynamic was reborn. Nature was alive and conscious and the body was wedded back to the "mind" in a new relation.

I began using Berman's book in my classes and it proved a better guide to the arguments in American poetry of the "Pound tradition" than the many critical histories of the period. Indeed, Berman had figured out the real poetics of Romanticism and of Modernism as a cry for the return of a squandered spirituality lost for five long centuries. James Hillman echoed Berman over an even wider canvas when he remarked in *Healing Fiction* (1994) that monotheism had robbed the mind of its many voices and gave it only one, a god who morphed into a devouring ego by the time we entered the Industrial Revolution. It gave him work as a therapist, he wryly noted, for the Christian era marked a great upwelling of mental illness, a point not lost on Berman's own history, or on the poets. Berman could stand outside the fields of poetry and psychotherapy and come to the same conclusions, free of the drag of conservative ideology that has made criticism of modern poetry often blind to its real implications.

But a turn away from the vast optimism of *Reenchantment* occurred later in the decade. As Berman noted to me in an e-mail, "I began to see the limits of a consciousness (or paradigm-shift) change during the 1980s." And in the decade following, he began writing *The Twilight of American Culture* (2000) in a state of shock at what was happening to American society from the go-go Reagan years to the Clinton era. "It was just that by the mid-90s I became aware of how public signs were misspelled, how data kept pouring in regarding the ignorance of the American public, and how cynical the nation had become."

A streamlined America with more leisure meant that learning the hard and slow way was heading south with the slide rule, the used book stores, art classes, the bearded intellectual as cultural anti-hero, with his tattered copy of *The Stranger* in his back pocket, or the girl with beads and rings reading *Fear and Trembling* on a park bench in

Washington Square. Corporate media were everywhere offering the homogeneous products of brand-name rock and roll, themed movies targeted at 18-30 year olds, fan mags, and fast food. More subtle erosions of self-reliance came with products that one couldn't fix, but simply replaced. Computer components made it impossible to tinker with a car anymore, or repair appliances. Shopping slowly replaced other modes of social life; the passive shopper consuming food and gadgets was adrift in a hypnotic trance of self-indulgence as Berman was typing out his jeremiad. After 9/11, Berman wrote a sequel to the *Twilight* book, *Dark Ages America* (2006), in which he argues that there is no turning around a culture bent on destroying itself. Threatened by these implications, Michiko Kakutani opened her hostile review of it in the *New York Times* by proclaiming, "This is a book that gives the Left a bad name." But a year later, Bob Herbert, an Op-Ed columnist for the same paper, wrote that "the country is going down the tubes . . . A country that refuses to properly educate its young or to maintain its physical plant is one that has clearly lost its way." "The end is near." Berman had already been there, said that.

With *Dark Ages* Berman had come full circle in his thinking. But as he told me recently, "One thing I need to emphasize is that the *Dark Ages* book ends on a note of optimism—not for the US, but for the human spirit, which I do believe always prevails. So I say that we (the US) are finished, but that the zeitgeist is moving on, and will show up in another place. Maybe Europe, with its plans for a renewed continent under a constitution; possibly even Latin America—Che Guevara's dream." As for Mexico, he noted, "I think that my collection of poems shows how vibrant life down here can be, how human."

If Berman has an antecedent from the previous generation, it is Paul Goodman, whose own vigorous condemnations of consumer society and deteriorating intelligence were argued in a similarly frank and clear-headed prose in *Gestalt Therapy* (1951) and *Growing Up Absurd* (1960). Goodman was passionate about learning, about discovery, about the self's need to expand its limits and embrace life at all levels. And he loved the balanced psyche poised between revelation and the dark irrational impulses flooding the back of the mind. But he reserved for his poetry his unbridled celebrations of life raw and direct, unmediated; his poems in *Hawkweed* (1967), like many of Berman's poems, were a retreat from the battleground of American disintegration. There he could revel in his own passions and pleasures and push away the gathering gloom he saw at the heart of the Vietnam War.

Berman's poems in *Counting Blessings* are rooted in the same pleasure principle. And while several of them register the decline of America, sunny, disheveled Mexico is everywhere in this book, thrusting its wedded vision of darkness and joy into every corner of his imagination. Just after finishing *Dark Ages America*, Berman moved south of the border, leaving America's blighted fortunes behind him. "I still miss the US, of course, New York especially – but all in all, I prefer to visit than to be embedded in it. The place was making me crazy, really, and to be free of all that endless hype and commercial noise—well, it's a huge relief. The land itself, however, will always be in my body."

> Sit in this café long enough
> and everyone you know will walk by.
> That's what they say, anyway.
> By what miracle did I shed the old life
> the life of autistic hostility
> and emerge, reborn, in a new place, a new time?

So opens the book, announcing its major theme – recovery from the battle, the lonely work of prophesying in a wilderness. Suddenly, whisked away to a country where the Reformation never happened, he can stop, collect himself, and watch

> A complicated, delicate insect
> crawling along the edge of a pot in my garden,
> delicate feelers, large green eyes
> absorbed in what it was doing.
> I can do that, once in a while:
> three seconds every month, perhaps.

Some of these poems go back to family history, his Jewish childhood in New York, for the poem is a dark chamber in which memory and recognition have their will. Things come out of privacy into a limpid, airy language, and find their way to us through the leisurely rhythms of conversation. Even religion comes up, for "writing poetry/ is the closest relationship one can have with God." Running through the poems is a basting stitch of simple happiness. After the dark books, the poems are full of quiet joy and gratitude, as in "Pentecost," whose epiphany is the lover in "black panties and high heels," putting on lipstick as she leans over the bathroom sink, causing him to slap his face and ask, "Is this really my life?"

Peeling back the layers of anxiety and condemnation leaves a natural self exposed, one in the act of recovering the silence, the peace of a terrace green with vines and potted plants, a blue sky overhead. The mind is reacquainted with the body, as in "The Mind-Body Problem," where the body is "saying over and over again:/I am your first love." D.H. Lawrence felt the same impulses restoring him to health in *Mornings in Mexico*, a brief sojourn in Mexico City while staying at the Monte Carlo Hotel. He poured himself into the sunlight and stretched out on his bed to enjoy the odors of burnt corn, ripe fruit, the sounds of the Mercado Merced down the street. These poems are no different, even though Berman, a recovering exile, is haunted by his past, his memories of small towns in upstate New York in the autumn. He feels the tug of his country.

"The Courtyard" is among my favorite of these lyric sketches. It is how exile should be conducted. Ovid at the Black Sea must have had such consolations once in a while as he awaited a change of heart from Augustus. This courtyard is "full of plants," a rosemary bush that "smells divine." It is "what I imagine heaven will be like."

> I plunk myself down in a wrought iron chair
> next to a wrought iron table
> (one covered with a pane of glass)
> and smoke a small cigar
> while I sit and read.

The poems are a kind of sketch pad for how one regains a life little by little from a culture that had wrapped its tentacles about you and squeezed out your breath. There is the slow process of putting oneself back together again, far from the screeching music of the television, the hard sell of the radio, the hysterical momentum of consumption as a stay against loneliness. All that abates as the exile sits in his bathrobe with a good book, a quiet heart. The reader who pores over these memories and observations will feel the ache to slip away to one's own courtyard in a foreign country, to sit and let the mind idle over its thoughts, to float back to the quiet and calm and, as Berman says, to count one's blessings.

To my family, now long gone:

Joseph
Dora
Barnett
Abe
Libbie
Ruby

TABLE OF CONTENTS

COUNTING BLESSINGS

. . . the earliest mode, the unqualified animal-poetic mode,
of erotic intercourse with the surround.

— Dorothy Dinnerstein, *The Mermaid and the Minotaur*

I learn by going where I have to go.

— Theodore Roethke, "The Waking"

Identity

Sit in this café long enough
and everyone you know will walk by.
That's what they say, anyway.
By what miracle did I shed the old life
the life of autistic hostility
and emerge, reborn, in a new place, a new time?
Of course, identity is identity:
you don't get a new shin bone.
There are days I miss my childhood,
Eastern Europe transplanted to the United States.
My grandfather above all,
with his halo of white hair
and his black, plastic-framed magnifying glass
poring over the Yiddish newspapers.
Or reading the *New York Times*,
then telling me what Sulzberger had to say that day.
A whole world of learning
expired when he died.

He did tell me how it started, though:
a *cheder* in White Russia
where the *rebbe* smeared *aleph* and *bet*
on his slate, in honey, for him to lick off,
at age five.
It flowed into his veins
then into my mother's
and here I sit,
120 years later and a million miles away,
writing poetry in this tiny café.

Ruby

An illustrious career, my uncle had:
spy in French West Africa
bodyguard to Churchill in Marrakech
foot soldier in the liberation of Rome.
A street dance: GI's lined up opposite Roman girls
as in a Virginia reel.
La donna è mobile.
Weaving in and out, one of them
presses the key to her apartment into my uncle's hand.
He came for the night, stayed for a year—
an old story; you know how it goes.
I was born during that time;
a few months later
Ruby saw a book, a children's fairy tale,
in a shop along the Via Flaminia
and went in and bought it.
Filastrocca, the story of a popular Italian folk hero,
written in the Torino dialect.
It came in the mail when I was a few months old.
"For Morris," Ruby had written,
"so that some day he will want to know many languages."

Ruby was a lodestar
though we never saw eye to eye on communism.
But underneath that rigidity,
a great sense of humor
that occasionally flashed when he let down his guard.
I sat beside him as he lay dying
far too soon, at sixty or so.
I held his hand as he tried to say my name
through the fog of morphine.

Because he was her kid brother
and she had to take care of him as a child,
my mother occasionally confused me with him.
"You remember when you and I and Pa-"
she would start.
"Ma," I would say gently, interrupting her,
"I'm your *son*."
She would become flustered and embarrassed,
afraid she was going senile...which might have been true.
Still, he meant a lot to both of us.

Occasionally I think of the two of us, Ruby and me,
meeting in heaven
sometime in the future
and catching up on the last fifty years.
What would I want to ask him,
of all the things I might?

"Rube, just one question:
Whatever happened to the Italian girl?"

A Prayer: To the God of Lost Causes

When my father died,
I did not appear in his obituary.
His wife was listed as surviving him
along with various nieces.
Then came the dog and cat,
and some beloved pieces of furniture.
In death, as in life,
I didn't exist.
"Good journalism," said one friend of mine.

Eight months later,
on the morning of my fifty-fourth birthday,
he came to me in a dream.
"You were right to keep knocking on the door,"
he said; "it's just that I couldn't answer.
Religion got the better of me," he went on;
"I was frozen, stuck in time."

I felt better, having the explanation.
Truth be told, I would rather have had the love.

The Fish

The rarest of things,
too amazing to believe:
my father decides to take me on a fishing trip
with a group of other men.
I mean, I'm seven years old, or thereabouts
and he has never spent time with me at all.
I'm excited, can hardly believe my luck.
I stand on the pier with my fishing rod in the water;
suddenly, a tug on the line.
I pull the rod upward,
reel the fish in,
and look on, horrified,
as I see that the hook is lodged in the fish's eye.
The lens comes out
to reveal coiled springs,
like those of a watch.
I lurch feebly to the edge of the pier and sit down,
my legs made of jelly.
I may have wept; I don't recall.
I can't remember what my father said,
or if he said anything at all.
We never went fishing again.

Not a Day at the Races

There really is no way to say it in words.
A cyclindrical, ceramic wastebasket
blue and white
squares and circles
or wasps in my garden.
Not the *ding an sich* (too Germanic)
but just–whatever it is.
Not fair! Not fair!
That the obvious is the most obscure.

Last Rites

They told me to stop and smell the roses.
I was never sure what that meant.
It was hard even in "retirement,"
though I did get better at it over time.
A complicated, delicate insect
crawling along the edge of a pot in my garden
delicate feelers, large green eyes
absorbed in what it was doing.
I can do that, once in a while:
three seconds every month, perhaps.
And don't tell me *la vida es sueño*;
I mean, Goya knew better than that.
It may be late in the day to discover all this
but I don't intend to spend the last few hours like Saturn,
devouring my own children.

Light

Light comes in
when a tectonic shift occurs,
so to speak.
Maybe it's in my family.
In the course of her divorce
my mother saw a burning bush.
No, I mean it, just like in the bible.
She ran home and lay down,
frightened out of her wits.
Her life had cracked open;
the burning bush entered that empty space.
Her therapist told her not to think about it–
end of story.

I recall a number of incidents like that in my own life,
some more "cosmic" than others.
One occurred on the way to school
when I was seven years old;
it was one of those rare February days in upstate New York
when the temperature soars and the snow begins to melt
and I was walking with two friends–
the light was all around me
as though I were in heaven.

There was another one at age fourteen
and then a major blowout at twenty-nine.
It took me three books to work that one out.
And around age sixty, perhaps a little before,
I saw a pillar of fire–again, as in the bible
and I began to weep.
This time it stuck:
I see it more or less every day now.
Exodus says it guided the Jews through the desert,
but I'm not looking for the Promised Land.
Oh no–
wandering in the desert *is* the Promised Land.

Ma

A little kid,
coming home from school at lunchtime
walking down the hill to my house.
It's spring, and the sun is shining,
and my mother is standing on the porch,
leaning on the railing,
smiling at me.
A sensation of love, purity, total security.
There is something about the light that seems holy;
I never saw light like that again until I was in Tuscany
fifteen or twenty years later.
In my memory, the scene appears as in a dream
bathed in a glow, or mist–
a kind of religious aura.

I smile back.

Ice

My mother's first epiphany
came at age ten
when the boat taking the family to America
put in temporarily at Antwerp.
None of the kids had ever eaten ice cream.
My grandfather bought everybody a cone
and said the word in Russian: *morozhenoe.*
For my mother, it became a magical word
associated with a taste that seemed to have descended from
       [heaven.
Morozhenoe. From the word for frost—*moroz.*
I buried her eighty-four years later
in a grave with a small tombstone
in upstate New York
in the middle of a snowstorm.
Frost lay on the ground.
When the rabbi read the 137th Psalm
I wept.
There were no epiphanies that day
just a single, stark recognition:
I would never, ever, see her again.

Reasons for Writing

Maybe writing poetry
is the closest relationship one can have with God.
Well, maybe not the closest,
but close enough.
What is God, after all,
but paying attention to the moment?
Proust taught us that most of our lives
are lived between anticipation and reflection—
as far as one can get from God, I suppose.
But then, staying in the present is not easy.
Maybe it's only infants who can inhabit the garden of Eden.
I do recall my first conscious moment, though,
my first memory, at age two and a half,
looking out through French louvre doors
onto a dull winter scene
and wondering if the world was a safe place to be.
The question pursued me all my life;
Yes and No was finally the best I could do.
I don't worry too much about it any more, thank God;
I just sit in my chair and write.

I Miss You

Letting go of love
when you have no choice
is a little like dying without morphine.
And then you realize–though you knew it before, of course–
that the closeness was not about sex
but about being able to take care of someone
without a thought for yourself.
"Our goal is not to make something happen,"
goes an old Gestalt saying;
"It's to see what actually does happen."
I found out.

Pentecost

There was a moment early in our relationship
that first weekend in the apartment on Connecticut Avenue
when I glimpsed you in the bathroom as I walked by,
leaning over the sink, carefully putting on your lipstick
and wearing nothing but black panties and high heels
and I slapped my face, as if to wake myself up
and said, almost aloud:
Is this really my life?
Was I a saint in a former life, then,
and is this my karma, in this one?
Or maybe it's true,
that all things come to those who stand and wait.

The Mind-Body Problem

Sometimes, the mind races far ahead of the body.
Most of my life has been like that.
I've spent a lot of time
being able to analyze that which I couldn't actually do.
I remember some kid in college
who was always relaxed,
always at home in his own skin.
He felt, to me, like an alien being;
I would have killed to have what he had.
There is such a thing as body genius:
Wayne Gretzky on the ice, for example,
anticipating an opening before it even shows up.
An extreme unself-consciousness,
like Jerry Seinfeld, or Steve Martin, say,
in front of a mike, working the crowd.
Sex is like that, of course,
and also, giving birth.
And once, for a brief moment, I had it
when I took a game off my tennis instructor,
a guy who had played professionally in his time.
It never happened again.
I mean, most of the time I'm just in my head
sailing along the waters of some great intellectual sea.
Nothing wrong with that.
Except, as John Finley once wrote,
there is always a pull within us,
something that wants "the clear signals of the senses,
by which alone the world is made fresh and definite."
He was talking about the Homeric Greeks,
the Greeks of *The Iliad*,
who were able to see reality without filters.
Later, a shadow fell across that perception;
this happens to children as well, as they grow up.

And yet the body always calls,
always beckons,
saying over and over again:
I am your first love.

Sabbatical

Weightlessness: the happiest time of my life.
Moving to Vancouver in the spring of 1985
putting my bed down amidst a forest of unpacked boxes
and sleeping for ten uninterrupted hours,
the sleep of the dead.
Free at last.
Time to write the book I had been thinking about
for several years now.
Seventeen uninterrupted months, without students, without
        [colleagues,
without those dreadful department meetings that seemed to go on
        [interminably.
An apartment on English Bay
shaped like a hexagon;
a skylight above the bed.
The light streams in every morning
and I get up,
make coffee,
put on the blue sweat suit I was to wear every day for the entire
        [year and a half.
I sit at my desk for four or five hours
immersed in work.
Then lunch, a nap, and a visit to the gym (no need to change
        [clothes);
Friends in the evening, maybe a movie;
then get up the next day and do it all over again.
A honeymoon with myself, with ideas, with the world.
The *sensuousness* of learning; the absorption of the craft.

But nostalgia can be a terrible thing.
If that was the high point of my life,
everything else was flat by comparison.

I returned to teaching in the fall of '86
and wasn't able to recapture the rush of my sabbatical
until 2006, twenty years later, when I finally "retired,"
left the rat race once and for all.
Not good.
I would sit and daydream, often, during those twenty years,
about "the time in Vancouver."
Nothing measured up to it;
it felt like my life was over.
The pain of knowing what life *could* be like
and not having it
is a difficult one to endure.
"Everything in moderation," said the ancient Greeks—
wise counsel from a wise people.
And yet the shamans of Thrace
and the Mysteries of Eleusis
were a constant temptation.
They knew all about the "divine madness,"
those oh-so-rational people.
The truth: everybody needs a little Vancouver,
now and then.

The Conspiracy

"The death instinct hovers over the United States,"
wrote some journalist a few years back.
It was a bad book with one good idea.
And I think: How did this happen?
Growing up in the fifties
we all had a different scenario in mind.
But you can't keep on doing bad things
and expect a good result.
When the crowds look at the death mask that was Reagan
and idolize him
you know we're on our last legs.
"There is no such thing as society,"
said Thatcher,
as she proceeded to kill it.
We didn't object.
We bought laptops and PlayStations and cell phones
and forgot our next-door neighbor's name.
Hell, we never even learned it in the first place.
Now we float in death and call it life
as the grim, psychotic face of Cheney
greets us on the television screen every day
Like a scene out of *1984*.
9/11 a conspiracy?
I'm not sure it really matters.

Die Mauer

I lived in Germany during the time that the Wall came down.
Heady days.
I remember early on, in 1989,
walking on the outskirts of Berlin with a German friend
back and forth, across the line in the sand
where the Wall recently stood.
It felt strange.
Some months later,
in the center of town,
near the Reichstag,
the locals were selling pieces of the Wall,
stained with brightly colored graffiti
and Russian army hats,
all the energy drained out of the once-powerful red star.
Checkpoint Charlie became a relic, a museum,
and *Ossis* poured across the once-lethal border,
intoxicated by the new freedom.
But what kind of freedom?
From the *Stasi*, to be sure,
and a paranoid regime minutely preoccupied with "the lives of others"
(like the United States today).
But the bulk of the excitement was over *Technik*,
the electronic toys suddenly available in abundant supply.
Turns out, the American model is an illusion as well–
sinnentleert, devoid of meaning.
How much freedom can one squeeze out of a DVD player, after all?

It's no use, finally;
we simply have to find a different way to live.

The Dodo Bird

Winter, 1992.
One of my students at the Gesamthochschule Kassel
wants to take me to a concert of Yiddish music
(I guess she figured out I was Jewish).
Two German-Jewish guys singing songs
they recovered from old manuscripts
hidden in various attics and basements
from all over Germany and Eastern Europe.
Who would come to this?, I wonder.
I'm guessing, twenty people at most.
Surely, Kassel doesn't want to remember its lost Jewish
        [population...
Although there is a commemorative plaque
just off the town square
marking the day that that population was *verschleppt*–
rounded up and dragged off to the concentration camps.
I wait to see what happens.
To my amazement, by the time the concert begins
on this frozen night, at 11:30 p.m.,
more than 150 *Kasseler* show up.
The hall is packed; the audience fills the aisles,
with people practically hanging from the ceiling.

The concert begins, and the audience remains perfectly still.
Plaintive old melodies fill the air;
I even recognize some of them from childhood,
or at least, that style of music,
and that old, crackling, agglutinated sound.
This ain't "Du liegst mir am Herzen," that's for sure.
No: this is my life; this is who I am.
But the respectful silence of the audience
slowly begins to feel uncomfortable.

The distance between it and the performers seems infinite,
   [somehow.
And then it hits me:
they think that they are witnessing an oddity,
a dead culture–
a dodo bird.
Indeed, I was the first Jew my landlady in Berlin (whom I dearly
   [love)
had ever laid eyes on,
and she was forty-two years old.
The atmosphere becomes increasingly creepy–
unheimlich, as Freud would have said.
I am on the verge of standing up, of shouting
(my German is pretty good by now):
"What do you think, you *Arschlöcher*,
that we are bugs on a slide?
That we are 'history'?
Let me tell you something, you *Scheissköpfe*–
we are not 'history',
we *make* history
and don't you forget it."
But I remain silent.
After all, I am a guest in this country
and some of my students at the Gesamthochschule
are undoubtedly in the audience.
Decorum must be preserved
even in the face of this bizarre "obituary."

Show over, I walk home in the sub-zero temperature,
the cold German night
seeping into every corner of my Jewish soul.

Philosophical Investigations

Wandering through Wittgenstein's house in Vienna
the one he built for his sister, Margarethe,
you can't help thinking:
this is the *Tractatus*,
in the form of a building.
I mean, it's so austere—
the masculine, Platonic lines
and the purely functional doorknobs.
Everything perfectly aligned, down to the last millimeter.
Wittgenstein did a complete flip in mid-life, of course,
deciding that the truth had to reside here on earth,
not in heaven.
Suddenly, it was all about context.
I wonder what *that* house would look like.
Couches with the stuffing coming out, maybe;
pigeons roosting on a window ledge
or even in the corner.
A few friends sleeping on the floor, perhaps,
clothes piled in a heap.
And lots of sex going on, too—
Platonists need not apply.
The first was a world without friction;
the second had nothing but.
Wittgenstein felt more at home in the second,
often entertaining his philosophy class at Cambridge
with examples from American detective stories.
But the first world refused to let him go;
there is, after all, something uncannily erotic about asceticism.
"The sense of the world must lie outside the world,"
he told a colleague the year before he died;
"in it there is no value,
it must lie outside all happening and being-so.

It must lie outside the world."
He died in 1951,
declaring that he had had a wonderful life.
Sometimes I picture him as a pure spirit
floating above the world
shyly wondering if he is, in fact, the meaning of it.

Liebe ist Arbeit

"Endlich muss man beginnen zu lieben," wrote Freud,
"um nicht krank zu werden"–
Finally one has to begin to love
in order not to become ill.
He had a way with words, he did,
the old sage of Vienna;
there's just no way of avoiding the truth.
Of course there are many things one can love:
an idea, God, a particular way of life, gardening.
It doesn't have to be romance.
Yet it was romance Freud was talking about,
that's clear enough.
Anthony Storr, the British psychiatrist,
argued that Freud nailed the twentieth century to a cross,
the cross of marriage as the only healthy way of life.
It's all a very modern idea, said Storr;
and it turns love into work, a "project," as it were.
Whereas in the Middle Ages,
a great many people fell in love
with an idea, God, or a particular way of life
and nobody thought anything of it;
there was no one right way to live.

I'm glad to hear it.
Myself, I'm in love with many things.
But I wasn't born and raised in a monastery;
I'm a modern, and my sacrament is a real flesh-and-blood partner,
one whom I can taste on my tongue.
But the odds are not good.
At the same time Freud declared health was marriage
the whole institution was starting to break down.
Or as Woody Allen once put it,

"people would rather hang on to their neuroses
than to their relationships."
Funny man with a sad message.
It reminds me of another funny man, my old friend,
Don Brodeur,
now gone,
an artist living in the Projects in San Francisco during the seventies,
and on whom I dropped in practically every day.
One day I arrived to find that he had nailed a bunch of cereal
        [boxes to the wall,
outside his door,
all in a row;
Special K, I think they were.
"Don, what is all this?" I asked him, a bit bewildered.
"Oh, that's my latest," he said rather proudly, waving his arm;
"I call it 'cereal monogamy'."

Suspended Animation

The days between the diagnosis
and the MRI
stretch out like eternity.
"Probably an operation," the doctor told me.
"I'm guessing a ruptured tendon."
I scan the Internet for information.
Tendon transfer (to a muscle)
four hours under the knife
two months, you'll barely be able to move
a year for recovery, all in all.
Suddenly, there's the world of activity
and the world of complete immobility,
a kind of death-in-life,
and you're hovering between the two of them
not knowing what will happen.

It feels a lot like a divorce,
when you have no place to stand
and you become strangely sensitive to the lives of others.
You hear what they say
their pain becomes real
you are aware of their lives from the inside
and this catches you by surprise.
A sixth sense, is what you suddenly feel you have.

Several days later, sitting in the radiology lab,
you read the technician's report.
"Severe inflammation," it says.
The word "rupture" does not appear.
The doctor talks about physical therapy;
there will be no cutting involved.

Slowly, the gap begins to close.
You still hear your friends, but with less intensity.
Ego begins to move back toward the center
until the empty space, the sixth sense,
becomes a distant memory.

Is walking along the edge of hell
the only way to be human?

¡Ahora!

At a museum in Nîmes, June 1988.
An exhibition of art dealing with bullfighting.
I am entranced by a painting by Descossy–
early twentieth century?–
showing a bull and matador, exhausted,
preparing for the showdown, the final encounter.
Both man and animal seem to understand
that all of this is fated: the moment of truth.
They eye each other warily, steadily;
frank recognition.
The sun is past the midpoint in the sky,
and casts long shadows of both figures on the ground.
The feeling is one of heat, stillness, and infinite clarity.
¡Ahora!–the title of the painting.
I stare at the canvas for a long time.
This must be what war is like, I think,
when you have to go into battle with the enemy
and know that only one of you is going to come out alive.
Or like any major challenge
anchored in a primal reality:
birth, love, terminal illness, death.
Time stands still; ¡Ahora! is the moment of the eternal now.
Don't kid yourself, my friend:
there really is such a thing as fate.

The Reunion

I sometimes imagine what it would be like,
a few years hence
to go to my fiftieth high school reunion.
As of today, I haven't quite made up my mind.
I mean, I'm guessing that the most interesting people,
the ones I would really like to see again,
won't show up.
Unlike myself, they've got better things to do.
I can't imagine it would be much fun:
after all, who enjoys high school?
Goethe said that adolescence was funny only in retrospect
but looking back, it doesn't seem funny at all.
A few teachers made it worthwhile
but when I left, at age eighteen,
I never saw any of my classmates again.
So I can only guess:
the captain of the football team,
an insurance salesman in a nearby suburb.
The class president,
an alcoholic on skid row.
The senior prom queen–every boy's masturbation fantasy–
now a mother of eight, and a hundred pounds overweight.
And then there's me
a slightly chubby intellectual, unmarried, without kids,
with no great stories to tell
except maybe a few adventures of the mind (or heart)
which are kind of hard to relate over martinis and canapés.
How many of us, I wonder,
would want to go back fifty years in time
and see if we couldn't do it again:
"right," this time,
like Kathleen Turner in *Peggy Sue Got Married*.
It didn't work; she found she couldn't alter her destiny.
But is there really such a thing as destiny?

Is it all written down in advance,
the Akashic records, or some such thing?
I was always a loner
and can't imagine this would be any different
as I sit in a corner,
sipping my martini,
and marveling at how I blinked my eyes
and fifty years went by–just like that.

Gringos

It's odd to see how the gringos
who come to this small Mexican town
behave like they're still living in L.A.
"You can take the man out of the country
but you can't take the country out of the man"–
as though an inner wall
protects them from life.
What is normal in the U.S.
looks like pathology down here.
Octavio Paz wrote that contact for the Mexican is communion;
for the American, contamination.
You wonder why we wind up exterminating everything in sight.
As for the inner wall
a Mexican friend said to me:
"but you have it as well."
I had to think about that.
Clearly, you don't shed old habits overnight.
I meet the other gringos here
exchange business cards with them
and agree that we simply must get together.
I never call them, and they never call me.
Lately, I've taken to using their business cards as dental floss.
The sharp corners are particularly good for rooting out stubborn
        [strands of tamale
or of chile, that get caught between your teeth.
Like Cortés, I avoid contamination.
Meanwhile, the feathered serpent hovers above me
an amused smile playing on its serpentine lips.

Bájale

Bájale, vive sin prisa
says an overhead sign on the road to León.
Slow down, live without hurry:
good advice.
If you think of your life as a backpacking expedition,
what's the rush?
It won't be all that different from what came before,
the next bend in the road,
and if it is, you'll handle it.
Gandhi said there was more to life than increasing its speed;
Nehru disagreed.
So now we've got a suit-and-tie India,
the India of "progress," "globalization,"
and a timeless India,
the India of the Ganges, of Shakti and Shiva.
"Progress toward what, and from what?", Scheler once asked.
Nobody seems interested in what the word really means.
"The one who dies with the most toys wins"–
that's what people really believe, amazingly enough.
Trouble is, you have to set that backpack down
before they let you into heaven.
Those are the rules.
As for hell:
Where do you think you've been all this time?

The End of Days

I guess there are some things you never get over.
College towns in central and upstate New York in October
when the countryside is Indian-summer still
and the air shimmers golden in the late afternoon.
Walking on beds of maple leaves
brilliant orange and red
as though they fell to earth
just for you.
I studied math at Cornell
but this was the real infinity
though I didn't quite know it at the time.

The U.S. was a different place back then;
there still really was a sense of hope.
I remember Meyer Abrams reading Keats
in Goldwyn Smith Hall
and thinking that I really might, one day,
touch the Grecian urn.
Or that the country, as a whole,
could embrace "negative capability."
Yeah, right, as my freshman class was fond of saying.

History had other plans for us.
Those "vast, impersonal forces" Eliot spoke of
overwhelmed us all.
Who could have grasped
in those naïve days of sixty-two and three
the depths of our solipsism, our repressed hostility?
No use blaming it on Johnson
or even on Reagan
ghoulish jokes though they were.
No...it was us,
who couldn't even find Vietnam on a map
who thought life was about station wagons

and frozen food
and fighting the "Russkies"
and hating anybody who was different,
anyone who had half a brain.
Us, who taught our kids
that education was about jobs
that the "good life" was about goods
and that it was worth spending billions to walk on the moon
when we couldn't even walk down the streets of Detroit and Chicago
without nervously looking over our shoulders.

The decades wore on...
Now one-fifth of the population thinks the sun revolves around
         [the earth
one-fourth feels it's OK to use violence in the pursuit of your goals
and one-half believes the Soviet Union was our enemy in World War II
and Germany our ally.
Almost none of us know we're Number One in the world
in rate of incarceration
antidepressant use
single-person dwellings
and square miles of shopping malls.
So we cheer phony wars–
unless we fail to win them, of course–
and more than half of us sit around waiting for Jesus Christ to return,
and "rapture" the true believers up to heaven.

These are your neighbors
I used to say to dwindling audiences across the country;
how do you feel about all this?
The few left who can still spell correctly
who know who Picasso was
who can define "molecule" and "sonnet"
who regard it as tragic
that so many kids cheat in school, show up drunk, insult their teachers—
these few oddballs shuffle out silently, morosely,
knowing that this is, indeed,
The End of Days.

Lalo

Driving to San Miguel with Lalo—
a monthly ritual I always enjoy.
I go there to pick up my mail;
he comes along for the ride.
He lived there for twenty years
smoking dope, dropping acid
when he wasn't teaching Spanish to gringos.
These days, he restricts himself to beer
which he drinks out of a coffee cup
as we bounce along the uneven road, riddled with topes.
He rattles on in Spanish
telling me stories of this and that.
Lately I've been able to catch about ninety percent of it.
I met him two years ago;
within two hours we were brothers, joined at the hip.
That kind of recognition doesn't happen very often,
but it happens—like falling in love.
I kid him that we are amantes,
which makes him nervous,
especially after two sales girls in a hat shop gave each other
        [knowing looks.
He lost the baseball cap I bought him that day,
probably on purpose.
It's no use, amigo, I tell him;
everybody knows something is up.

Oly

My insurance agent wore a black slip to our first appointment.
When she bent over, her breasts nearly spilled out.
My girlfriend in Boston, when I told her the story,
wondered if Olivia wore a business suit to bed.
But Wen wasn't jealous.
"She's thirty years old, a bit pudgy, and wears too much makeup,"
I reassured her over the phone (just in case).
Guys her age, however, were definitely interested.
Even without the slip, Oly always affected a Latina siren persona:
tight black dress, platform shoes, red lipstick so incandescent
you needed sunglasses just to look at her.
I saw a lot of her over the next year;
I guess I had a lot of insurance business to transact.
She asked me questions about the English language
and would complain that she was too fat.
I finally figured it out:
underneath all the glamor,
she was an innocent.
But more than that, really...
When my ankle got inflamed, and a possible operation loomed,
and I needed insurance coverage for the mounting bills,
Oly made out the forms for me
went to the doctors with me
helped me get the right receipts from the pharmacist.
She didn't have to do any of this.
Last Christmas,
when I had to go to the hospital yet one more time for physical therapy,
she insisted on meeting me after the session
for an abrazo, a Feliz Navidad.
She never wanted a thing from me.
Who woulda thunk it?
Under a black slip,
a heart of gold.

Doctora Susana

"Come on, you'll love it,"
my acupuncturist tells me,
as she shoves a Bach flower remedy in my face.
"It'll open up your heart chakra."
Three days later, my guts are hanging out,
and I can't seem to shove them back in.
"This is too much," I tell her over the phone;
"what the hell was in that stuff?"
"Oh, walnut," she says
"and something else, I forget."
"I've gotta pull back," I tell her;
"I'm giving book tours.
I can't have my heart on my sleeve,
weeping during interviews, for Chrissakes."
"You need to flush out your emotions," she insists.
"I'm flushed!" I tell her;
"if I were any more flushed I'd be a toilet."
"Oh, don't be so dramatic," she says.
"OK, switch to Rescue Remedy for a while."
I follow her instructions, return to normal.
The lecture series goes well.
"How together that guy is," everybody says;
"how completely in control of himself."

Curriculum Vitae

My c.v. is twenty-five pages long.
Printed out, it would probably weigh about two pounds.
I don't know why I bother keeping it up to date.
I mean, I'll never apply for another job.
I guess it's a record, of sorts,
a detailed list of what I did, and when and where I did it.
It exists only in my computer, however;
I never bothered to print a hard copy out.
One crash, and my entire life would go up in smoke–
a form of Russian roulette.
About once a month
I summon it up on the screen
and tinker with the fine details:
line up the margins (always in disrepair)
extract a comma
replace a colon with a dash.
It's sort of like primping in front of a mirror,
an exercise in vanity.
One day, I'll either have to print it out
or gather up my courage and hit Delete.
For now, I remain postmodern:
a virtual identity is the best I can do.

New Age Guru

She is about sixty pounds overweight
and looks like a beached whale.
Yet her empty platitudes hold the audience spellbound,
disciples desperate for an answer.
She gives it to them: it's me, she says.
They are enthralled as she lectures to them for ninety minutes
on how she finally managed to transcend her ego.
Is this what Fascism is like?, I wonder.
I don't have long to wait.
Her sermon over, she soon has her audience,
a hundred or so in all,
marching around the room in a trance.
She leans over to me and whispers, conspiratorially,
"I'd like to do this with twenty thousand people."
I shrug. "No need," I tell her;
"it's already been done."
She stares at me blankly.
"*Auf wiedersehen*," I say,
taking my leave.

Communication

The day after I put up a sign outside my door,
about No Throwing Garbage Here,
dog turds appear beneath it.
One can never tell in Mexico:
Innocent, or a message?
It really could be either.
Of course on Friday nights
it's just weekend revelry.
I wake up on Saturday,
go outside,
and pick up the empty packets of taco chips,
the Coke cans,
the broken glass.
I know, it's a small price to pay for living here,
in a place this gracious,
on a street this quiet,
in a house this beautiful.
But there remains something stubborn and irreducible about dog turds,
no matter how cleverly you try to rationalize them away.
I'm just not able to give them a positive spin.
They are concrete, have texture,
and sit there looking at me,
communicating something (go fuck yourself)
or nothing at all (hey, we're just a bunch of turds).
The same thing happened in the midst of a major festival last month
when someone threw a bamboo cross into my courtyard.
I put it down to holiday celebration, but who knows?
Maybe the message was: How come we don't see you in church?
For now, I'll live with the turds.
There is something about ambiguity I find downright intriguing.

Deep Breathing

"As our souls, being air, hold us together," wrote Anaximenes,
"so breath and air embrace the entire universe."
It seems plausible.
The second sentence of Genesis tells us that *ruach elohim merachefet*
       [*al pnei hamayim*—
the breath of God hovered over the face of the water.
I sometimes wonder what it would be like
to live in that Void
before the Creation,
before anything inhabited the earth.
To float on the water,
feeling the breath of God on my face,
or even, to see His.
I think of my father's face like that
except it would be a lot sadder.
Hard to get up, get ready for the Creation,
when you know what the next few decades are going to be like.
Not that any of us have a choice.
Me, I had to be extracted with forceps:
I knew this life thing wasn't going to be a whole lot of fun.
And yet, I'm in no hurry to return...
There's so much sweetness in a single day
a single woman
a single hummingbird
a single fountain pen
a single poem.

The Courtyard

Sitting in the small courtyard that adjoins my house
is sometimes what I imagine heaven will be like.
I do it nearly every morning.
It's full of plants—
some of them quite tall—
and one occasionally puts forth deep purple flowers
more royal than the king's robe in ancient Egypt,
or maybe it was the emperor's in Rome, I forget.
The outside wall has no doorbell
but rather an actual bell, on a chain,
hanging in a kind of grotto,
the kind you might see in a *campanile* in Italy
or on display in Philadelphia
only much smaller, of course.
It's a ritual, after breakfast:
I plunk myself down in a wrought iron chair
next to a wrought iron table (one covered with a pane of glass)
and smoke a small cigar
while I sit and read.
Occasionally, someone rings the bell:
"¡Agua Ciel!" he cries
and I get up, and tell him
"no, gracias; tengo suficiente."
There is also a sculpted rosemary bush
that smells divine.
I can sit there all day, if I want,
in my bathrobe (the neighbors from across the street
looking down at me, from their upstairs apartment)
but eventually I get up,
water the plants,
go back inside,
and get dressed.

Sometimes I wonder who will inherit the house—
a friend, a lover—
and whether they will sit in the very same chair,
and look at the very same plants.
Of course, I plan to live to a ripe old age
having read, some years ago, Irving Berlin's obituary
and thinking I too could make it to 101.
Hopefully my Spanish will be better by then.
But if the nurse asks me,
as I'm about to wink out,
if I want more life,
I hope I'll just smile
and tell her as gently as I can,
"no, gracias; tengo suficiente."

ABOUT THE AUTHOR

Morris Berman is well known as an innovative cultural historian and social critic. He has taught at a number of universities in Europe and North America, and has held visiting endowed chairs at Incarnate Word College (San Antonio), the University of New Mexico, and Weber State University. Between 1982 and 1988 he was the Lansdowne Professor in the History of Science at the University of Victoria, British Columbia. Berman won the Governor's Writers Award for Washington State in 1990, and was the first recipient of the annual Rollo May Center Grant for Humanistic Studies in 1992. In 2000 *The Twilight of American Culture* was named a "Notable Book" by the *New York Times Book Review*, and in 2013 he received the Neil Postman Award for Career Achievement in Public Intellectual Activity from the Media Ecology Association. Other published work includes *Dark Ages America* (2006), *A Question of Values* (2010), *Destiny* (2011), *Why America Failed* (2011), *Spinning Straw Into Gold* (2013), *Neurotic Beauty* (2015), *The Man Without Qualities* (2016), and a trilogy on the evolution of human consciousness: *The Reenchantment of the World* (1981), *Coming to Our Senses* (1989), and *Wandering God: A Study in Nomadic Spirituality* (2000). During 2003–6 he was Visiting Professor in Sociology at the Catholic University of America in Washington, D.C., and Visiting Professor in Humanities at the Tecnológico de Monterrey, Mexico City, during 2008–9. He lives in Mexico.

ALSO AVAILABLE FROM
THE OLIVER ARTS & OPEN PRESS

FICTION

THE MAN WITHOUT QUALITIES, Novel by Morris Berman (2016)t

THE DECLINE AND FALL OF THE AMERICAN NATION, Novel by Eric Larsen (2013)

THE END OF THE 19TH CENTURY, Novel by Eric Larsen (2012)

THE BLUE RENTAL, Texts by Barbara Mor, (2011)

ABLONG, Novel by Alan Salant (2010)

KIMCHEE DAYS, Novel by Timothy Gatto (2010)

TOPIARY, A Modular Novel by Adam Engel (2009)

NONFICTION

DANCE WITHOUT STEPS, Memoir by Paul Bendix (2012)

THE SKULL OF YORICK, Essays on the Cover-up of 9/11 by Eric Larsen (2011)

AFGHANISTAN: A WINDOW ON THE TRAGEDY, by Alen Silva (2011)

I HOPE MY CORPSE GIVES YOU THE PLAGUE, Essays by Adam Engel (2010)

HOMER FOR REAL: A READING OF THE ILIAD by Eric Larsen (2009)

FROM COMPLICITY TO CONTEMPT, Essays by Timothy Gatto (2009)

POETRY

A CROW'S DREAM, Poetry by Douglas Valentine (2012)

LISTENING TO THE THUNDER, Poems by Helen Tzagoloff (2012)

THE EXPEDITION SETS OUT, Poetry by Alan Salant (2011)

AUTUMN LAMP IN RAIN, Poetry by Han Glassman (2011)

PROSE CARTOONS

/ (ROOT), Prose Cartoons by Adam Engel (2016)

CELLA FANTASTIK, Prose Cartoons by Adam Engel (2011)

Oliver titles are available
through any bookseller or at
oliveropenpress.com

Lightning Source UK Ltd.
Milton Keynes UK
UKHW02f0654061217
313971UK00011B/794/P